Web Api and Security

INTERVIEW QUESTION AND ANSWERS

Copyrights

Web Api and Security Interview Question and Answers

About the Book

Web Api and Security interview questions is designed to help readers learn the basic concepts of Web Api.

This book covers all the concepts of Web Api and security with the help of Interview question and Answers.

Contents

Q1. What is Web Api ?

API stands for **A**pplication **P**rogramming **I**nterface.

The ASP.NET Web API is an extensible framework for building HTTP based services that can be accessed in different applications on different platforms such as web, windows, mobile etc.

It works more or less the same way as ASP.NET MVC web application except that it sends data as a response instead of html view.

Q2. What are Restful services ?

- RESTful Web Services are basically REST Architecture based Web Services.
- In REST Architecture **_everything is a resource_**.
- RESTful web services are light weight, highly scalable and maintainable and are very commonly used to create APIs for web-based applications
- REST are **_stateless_** and separate the concerns of client and server.

Q3. How REST is stateless ?

- REST are stateless, meaning that the server does not need to know anything about what state the client is in and vice versa.
- This constraint of statelessness is enforced through the use of _resources_, rather than _commands_.
- These constraints help RESTful applications achieve reliability, quick performance, and scalability.

Q4. What are Rest Api Architectural constraints ?

REST defines **6 architectural constraints** which make any web service – a true RESTful API.

1. **Uniform Interface:** It suggests that there should be an uniform way of interacting with a given server irrespective of device or type of application

(website, mobile app). Individual resources are identified in requests. For example: API/users.

2. **Stateless:** It means that the necessary state to handle the request is contained within the request itself and server would not store anything related to the session

3. **Cacheable:** Every response should include whether the response is cacheable or not and for how much duration responses can be cached at the client side.A caching eliminates some client–server interactions, improving performance.

4. **Client-Server:** A Client is someone who is requesting resources and are not concerned with data storage, which remains internal to each server, and server is someone who holds the resources and are not concerned with the user interface or user state. They can evolve independently.

5. **Layered system:** REST allows you to use a layered system architecture where you deploy the APIs on server A, and store data on server B and authenticate requests in Server C, for example. A client cannot ordinarily tell whether it is connected directly to the end server or an intermediary along the way.

6. **Code on demand(optional):** Most of the time, you will be sending the static representations of resources in the form of XML or JSON. But when you need to, you are free to return executable code to support a part of your application, e.g., clients may call your API to get a UI widget rendering code.

Q5. What is difference between wcf and api ?

WCF	API
It supports HTTP, TCP, UDP, and custom transport protocol.	It supports only the HTTP protocol.
It uses attributes based programming model.	Maps HTTP verbs to methods.
It uses Service, Operation, and Data contracts.	It uses a routing and controller concept similar to ASP.NET MVC.
It supports Reliable Messaging and Transactions.	It does not support Reliable Messaging and transactions.
It supports RESTful services but with limitations.	Ideal for building RESTful services.
WCF does not support MVC features	ASP.NET Web API supports MVC

like controllers, routing, filter, auction results, etc.	features such as routing, controllers, results, filter, action, etc.

Q6. When to choose WCF ?

You can choose WCF if your service needs to support multiple protocols such as HTTP, TCP, Named pipe.

Creating services that are transport/protocol independent. Single service with multiple end points (like .net, java etc.)

Q7. Explain breifly about request verbs, header, body ?

Request verbs(GET, POST, PUT, DELETE) : These verbs are used to define the functionalities of a resource.

Request Header : contains additional information about the request e.g. what type of response is required e.g. xml response, json response

Request body : contains the data to send to the server

Response body : contains the data sent as response from the server

Response status codes : provide the client, the status of the request.

e.g. 200 – status OK,

404 – not found

204 – no content

Etc.

Q8. What is API content Negotiation ?

- In REST clients can specify the types of response they want from server. For e.g. if they wants a response in xml format or json format etc.
- Using accept-header client can specify format they want from server

e.g.

[Request Header - xml format]

Accept : application/xml [client wants response in XML format]

[Response Header - xml format]

Content-Type: application/xml; charset=utf-8 [Content-type in response header will also be set as application/xml]

[Request Header - json format]

Accept: application/json [client wants response in JSON format]

[Response Header - json format]

Content-Type: application/json; charset=utf-8 [Content-type in response header will also be set as application/ json]

- According to Accept-header value in request header server sends response, this is known as **Content Negotiation.**
- Depending on request format, Api chooses an appropriate formatter.
- If client requested a xml data then Api chooses xml formatter or json formatter in case of json request. This formatter are classes and known as **Media Type Formatters**
- we can also specify multiple values for accept-header

e.g. Accept : application/xml,application/json

Note* : if Accept header is not specified, then ***by default Web Api return JSON data***

Q9. How can you change the settings of these formatters ?

if you want the JSON data to be properly indented : -

[WebApiConfig.cs file in App_Start folder]

config.Formatters.JsonFormatter.SerializerSettings.Formatting = Newtonsoft.Json.Formatting.Indented;

Use camel case instead of pascal case for property names

[WebApiConfig.cs file in App_Start folder]

config.Formatters.JsonFormatter.SerializerSettings.ContractResolver = new
CamelCasePropertyNamesContractResolver();

Q10. What is MediaTypeFormatter ?

- If client requested a xml data then Api chooses xml formatter or json
  formatter in case of json request to return a specified type of response.
  This formatter are classes and known as **Media Type Formatters**
- *MediaTypeFormatter* is an *abstract class* from which
  JsonMediaTypeFormatter and *XmlMediaTypeFormatter* classes inherit
  from. JsonMediaTypeFormatter handles JSON and XmlMediaTypeFormatter
  handles XML.

Q11. How to return only JSON/XML from Web API Service irrespective of the Accept header value ?

Using following code, irrespective of the Accept header value (application/xml or
application/json), the Web API service is always going to return JSON or XML : -

[WebApiConfig.cs – Register()]

// to accept JSON only :

config.Formatters.Remove(config.Formatters.XmlFormatter)

//to accept XML only :

config.Formatters.Remove(config.Formatters.JsonFormatter);

Q12. How to add custom formatter ?

Step 1 : you can add custom formatter class in WebApiconfig.cs

[WebApiConfig.cs]

```csharp
public class CustomJsonFormatter : JsonMediaTypeFormatter
{
public CustomJsonFormatter()
{
this.SupportedMediaTypes.Add(new MediaTypeHeaderValue("text/html"));
}
public override void SetDefaultContentHeaders(Type type, HttpContentHeaders headers, MediaTypeHeaderValue mediaType)
{
base.SetDefaultContentHeaders(type, headers, mediaType);
headers.ContentType = new MediaTypeHeaderValue("application/json");
}
}
```

Step 2 : Now, you need to register the custom formatter in WebApiConfig.cs

[WebApiConfig.cs – Register()]

```csharp
config.Formatters.Add(new CustomJsonFormatter());
```


Q13. What is [FromBody] attribute ?

- The parameter is decorated with [FromBody] attribute.
- This tells Web API to get data from the request body.

e.g.

```csharp
public void Post([FromBody] Employee employee)
```


Q14. How to return Response Messages in POST/GET request ?

```csharp
public HttpResponseMessage Post([FromBody] ModelName obj)
```

```
{

try

{

//TODO: db operations

var message = Request.CreateResponse(HttpStatusCode.Created, obj);

message.Headers.Location = new Uri(Request.RequestUri );

return message;

}

}

catch (Exception ex)

{

return Request.CreateErrorResponse(HttpStatusCode.BadRequest, ex);

}

}
```

Q15. Tell about Default conventions used by API to map methods ?

- By default, the HTTP verb GET is mapped to a method in a controller that has the name Get() or prefixed with the word Get
- The word *Get is case-insensitive*. It can be lowercase, uppercase or a mix of both.
- If the method is not named Get or if it does not start with the word get then Web API does not know the method name to which the GET request must be mapped and the request fails with an error message (status code 405 : Method Not Allowed)
- To instruct Web API to map HTTP verb GET to custom method which is not having Get prefixed to it, decorate the method with **[HttpGet]** attribute.

Q16. How to use Query string parameter in Api ?

Query string parameter can be passed in following way :

http://localhost/api/controllerName?branch=All

e.g.

```csharp
public HttpResponseMessage Get(string branch = "All")
{
    using (StudentDBEntities entities = new StudentDBEntities ())
    {
        switch (branch.ToLower())
        {
            case "all":
                return Request.CreateResponse(HttpStatusCode.OK, entities.Students.ToList());
            case "cs":
                return Request.CreateResponse(HttpStatusCode.OK,
                    entities. Students.Where(e => e.Branch.ToLower() == "cs").ToList());
            case "it":
                return Request.CreateResponse(HttpStatusCode.OK,
                    entities. Students.Where(e => e. Branch.ToLower() == "it").ToList());
            default:
                return Request.CreateErrorResponse(HttpStatusCode.BadRequest,
                    "invalid branch value");
        }
    }
}
```

Q17. What is the use of FromBody and FromUri attributes ?

The default convention used by Web API for **binding parameters : -**

- If the parameter is a **simple type** like int, bool, double, etc., Web API tries to get the value from the **URI** (Either from route data or **Query String**)
- If the parameter is a **complex type** like custom classes objects etc., Web API tries to get the value from the **request body**
- We can change this default parameter binding process by using [**FromBody**] and [**FromUri**] attributes.

e.g.

public HttpResponseMessage Put([**FromBody**]int id, [**FromUri**]Student obj)

Now, in the above example API will look for first simple parameter 'id' in request body and second complex parameter in a URI i.e.query string.

Q18. How to call ASP.NET Web API Service using jQuery ?

If both the client (i.e Html) and Api service are in same project than ajax calls can be used in jquery otherwise in different projects this will not work.

e.g.

// Ajax call in a Jquery

$(document).ready(function () {

$('#btn').click(function () {

$.ajax({

type: 'GET',

url: "api/controllerName/",

dataType: 'json',

success: function (data) {

```
$.each(data, function (index, val) {

//Todo

});

}

});

});
```


Q19. What is Attribute routing ?

Using the [Route] attribute to define routes is called Attribute Routing.

Advantages of using Attribute Routing

Attribute routing gives us more control over the URIs than convention-based routing. Creating URI patterns like hierarchies of resources (For example, students have courses, Departments have employees) is very difficult with convention-based routing. With attribute routing all you have to do is use the [Route] attribute as shown below.

[**Route**("api/students/{id}/courses")]

Enabling Attribute routing :

In ASP.NET Web API 2, Attribute Routing is enabled by default. The following line of code in WebApiConfig.cs file enables Attribute Routing.

[WebApiConfig.cs]
config.MapHttpAttributeRoutes();

Q20. Can we use both Attribute Routing and Convention-based routing in a single Web API project ?

Yes, both the routing mechanisms can be combined in a single Web API project.

The controller action methods that have the [Route] attribute uses Attribute Routing, and the others without [Route] attribute uses Convention-based routing.

Q21. What is the use of RoutePrefix attribute ?

RoutePrefix attribute is used to specify the **common route prefix** at the controller level to eliminate the need to repeat that common route prefix on every controller action method.

e.g.

```
public class StudentsController : ApiController
{
    [Route("api/students")]
    public IEnumerable<Student> Get()

    [Route("api/students/{id}")]
    public Student Get(int id)



    [Route("api/students/{id}/courses")]
    public IEnumerable<string> GetStudentCourses(int id)
}
```

The common prefix "api/students" can be specified for the entire controller using the [RoutePrefix] attribute as shown below.

```
[RoutePrefix("api/students")]
public class StudentsController : ApiController
{
    [Route("")]// path : "/api/students"
    public IEnumerable<Student> Get()

    [Route("{id}")]// path : "/api/students/{id}"
    public Student Get(int id)

    [Route("{id}/courses")]  // path : "/api/students/{id}/courses"
    public IEnumerable<string> GetStudentCourses(int id)
}
```

Q22. How to override the route prefix ?

Use ~ character to override the route prefix. Sometimes you may want to override the route prefix.

e.g.

```
[RoutePrefix("api/students")]
public class StudentsController : ApiController
{

   [Route("")]// path : "/api/ students "
   public IEnumerable<Student> Get()


   [Route("{id}")] // path : "/api/students/{id}"
   public Student Get(int id)


[Route("~/api/teachers")] // path : "/api/teachers"
public IEnumerable<Teacher> GetTeachers()
}
```

Q23. What are Route Constraints ?

```
[Route("api/students/{id}")]
public Student Get(int id)
{
return students.FirstOrDefault(s => s.Id == id);
}


[Route("api/students/{{name}")]
public Student Get(string name)
{
return students.FirstOrDefault(s => s.Name.ToLower() == name.ToLower());
}
}
```
//result : Error

At this point build the solution, and if you navigate to either of the following URI's you get an error stating "Multiple actions were found that match the request"

/api/students/1
/api/students/Mike

This is because the framework does not know which version of the Get() method to use. This is where constraints are very useful.

This can be very easily achieved using **Route Constraints** as shown below. To specify route constraint, the **syntax is "{parameter:constraint}".**

Some of the commonly used constraints are :

- Int
- Alpha(string - stands for uppercase or lowercase alphabet characters.)
- decimal
- double
- float
- long
- bool

e.g.

```
[Route("{id:int}")]
public Student Get(int id)
{
    return students.FirstOrDefault(s => s.Id == id);
}
```

```
[Route("{name:alpha}")]
public Student Get(string name)
{
    return students.FirstOrDefault(s => s.Name.ToLower() == name.ToLower());
}
```

Some of the constraints take arguments. To specify arguments use parentheses as shown below.

Constraint	Description	Example
min	Matches an integer with a minimum value	{x:min(0)}
max	Matches an integer with a maximum value	{x:max(100)}

length	Matches a string with the specified length or within a specified range of lengths	{x:length(3)} {x:length(1,10)}
minlength	Matches a string with a minimum length	{x:minlength(1)}
maxlength	Matches a string with a maximum length	{x:maxlength(100)}
range	Matches an integer within a range of values	{x:range(1,100)}

e.g.

- [Route("{id:int:min(1)}")]
- [Route("{id:int:min(1):max(3)}")]
- [Route("{id:int:range(1,3)}")]

WebApi Security

Q24. What is same origin policy ?

Browsers allow a web page to make AJAX requests only with in the same domain. Browser security prevents a web page from making AJAX requests to another domain. This is called same origin policy.

e.g.

The following 2 URLs have the same origin

http://localhost:8080/api/students

http://localhost:8080/students.html

The following 2 URLs have different origins, because they have different port numbers (8080 / 5000)

http://localhost:8080/ api/students

http://localhost:5000/Employees.html

The following 2 URLs have different origins, because they have different domains (.com / net)

http://localhost.com/api/students

http://localhost.net/students.html

The following 2 URLs have different origins, because they have different schemes (http / https)

http://localhost.com/api/students

https://localhost.net/students.html

Q25. What will happen if you make a Ajax call to cross domain ?

If we try to initiate a cross-domain request then we will get following error in a browser : -

[Error] : -

XMLHttpRequest cannot load http://localhost:8080/api/Students. No 'Access-Control-Allow-Origin' header is present on the requested resource. Origin 'http://localhost:5000' is therefore not allowed access.

Q26. What is CORS?

CORS stands for **Cross-Origin Resource Sharing**. It is a mechanism that allows restricted resources on a web page to be requested from another domain, outside the domain from which the resource originated. For security reasons, browsers restrict cross-origin HTTP requests initiated from within.

Q27. How to get solve the cross domain ajax problem ?

There are 2 ways to get around this problem

1. Using **JSONP** (JSON with Padding)
2. Enabling **CORS** (Cross Origin Resource Sharing)

Q28. what is JSONP and what does it do?

JSONP stands for JSON with Padding. All JSONP does is wraps the data in a function. So for example, if you have the following JSON object

```
{
  "FirstName" : "Steve",
  "LastName"  : "Anderson",
  "Gender"    : "Male",
}
```

JSONP will wrap the data in a function as shown below

```
CallbackFunction({
  "FirstName" : " Steve ",
  "LastName"  : " Anderson ",
  "Gender"    : "Male",
})
```

Browsers allow to consume JavaScript that is present in a different domain but not data. Since the data is wrapped in a JavaScript function, this can be consumed by a web page that is present in a different domain.

Q29. what are steps to use JSONP in Web Api ?

Steps to make ASP.NET Web API Service to return JSONP formatted data and consume it from a cross domain ajax request

Step 1 : To support JSONP format, execute the following command using NuGet Package Manager Console which installs WebApiContrib.Formatting.Jsonp package.

Install-Package WebApiContrib.Formatting.Jsonp

Step 2 : Include the following 2 lines of code in Register() method of WebApiConfig class in WebApiConfig.cs file in App_Start folder

```
var jsonpFormatter = new
JsonpMediaTypeFormatter(config.Formatters.JsonFormatter);

config.Formatters.Insert(0, jsonpFormatter);
```

Step 3 : In the ClientApplication, set the dataType option of the jQuery ajax function to jsonp

dataType: 'jsonp'

CORS - (Cross Origin Resource Sharing) – Allows cross-domain resource sharing

Steps to allow cross domain ajax calls by enabling CORS :

Step 1 : Install Microsoft.AspNet.WebApi.Cors package. Execute the following command using NuGet Package Manager Console.

Install-Package Microsoft.AspNet.WebApi.Cors

Step 2 : Enable CORS at Global Level :

Include the following 2 lines of code in Register() method of WebApiConfig class in WebApiConfig.cs file in App_Start folder

// this will enable CORS for all domains (*) at Global Level

 [WebApiConfig.cs]

EnableCorsAttribute cors = new EnableCorsAttribute("*", "*", "*");

config.EnableCors();

Parameters of EnableCorsAttribute : -

EnableCorsAttribute has 3 parameters : -

1. **Origins** : Comma-separated list of origins that are allowed to access the resource. For example "**http://www.localhost:8080 , http://www.localhost:5000** " will only allow ajax calls from these 2 websites. All the others will be blocked. Use "*" to allow all
2. **Header** : Comma-separated list of headers that are supported by the resource. For example "**accept,content-type,origin**" will only allow these 3 headers. Use "*" to allow all. Use null or empty string to allow none
3. **Method** : Comma-separated list of methods that are supported by the resource. For example "**GET,POST**" only allows Get and Post and blocks the

rest of the methods. Use "*" to allow all. Use null or empty string to allow none.

Q31. How to enable CORS at controller or action level only ?

Steps to enable CORS at Controller or Action methods level :

Step 1 : Install Microsoft.AspNet.WebApi.Cors package. Execute the following command using NuGet Package Manager Console.

Install-Package Microsoft.AspNet.WebApi.Cors

Step 2 : Enable CORS Controller or Action methods level :

Include the following code in Register() method of WebApiConfig class in WebApiConfig.cs file in App_Start folder

 [WebApiConfig.cs]

config.EnableCors();

Step 3 : If applied at a controller level then it is applicable for all methods in the controller. To apply it at the controller level :

Apply the EnableCorsAttribute on the controller class

[EnableCorsAttribute("*", "*", "*")]

public class StudentsController : ApiController

{

//Todo :

}

Same attribute can be applied at Action method as well.

Q32. Can we disable CORS for particular Action method as well ?

To disable CORS for a specific action apply [DisableCors] on that specific action.

Q33. What is purpose of Access-Control-Allow-Origin in CORS ?

When CORS is enabled, the browser sets the origin header of the request to the domain of the site making the request. The server sets Access-Control-Allow-Origin header in the response to either * or the origin that made the request. * indicates any site is allowed to make the request.

Q34. How to enable SSL in Visual Studio ?

Steps to enable SSL are :

1. In the Solution Explorer click on project and press F4 key on the keyboard. This launches Project Properties window.

2. In the Properties window, set SSL Enabled property to true. As soon as we do this Visual Studio sets SSL URL

```
⊟ Development Server
    Always Start When Deb  True
    Anonymous Authentica   Enabled
    Managed Pipeline Mod    Integrated
    SSL Enabled            True
    SSL URL               https://localhost:44341/
    URL                   http://localhost:58857/
    Windows Authenticatio  Disabled
```


Q35. Where can we store tokens in browser ?

We can store tokens in browser storage :

- **Session storage :** By closing the browser window. Since we are storing the access token in browser session storage, the access token will be lost when we close the browser window. [**sessionStorage** object is used]
- **Local storage:** If you do not want to loose the access token, when the browser is closed store the access token in browser local storage instead of session storage.[**localStorage** object is used]

Q36. Why We Need token based authentication?

- **Token-based authentication** is predominantly used on the web because it allows users to stay logged onto a website **without the use of cookies**.
- In addition to a more user-friendly experience, **tokens are more secure** because they can be used to replace a user's actual credentials.

Q37. How token based authentication actually works?

- In the Token based approach, the client application first sends a request to Authentication server endpoint with an appropriate credential.
- Now If the username and password are found correct then the **Authentication server send a token to the client as a response**.
- This token contains enough data to identify a particular user and an expiry time.The client application then uses the token to access the restricted resources in next requests till the token is valid.

Q38. Benefit of token authentication ?

- **Scalability of Servers**: The token sent to the server is self contained which holds all the user information needed for authentication, so adding more servers to your web farm is an easy task, there is no dependent on shared session stores.
- **Loosely Coupling**: Your front-end application is not coupled with specific authentication mechanism, the token is generated from the server and your API is built in a way to understand this token and do the authentication.
- **Mobile Friendly**: Cookies and browsers like each other, but storing cookies on native platforms (Android, iOS, Windows Phone) is not a trivial task, having standard way to authenticate users will simplify our life if we decided to consume the back-end API from native applications.

Q39. What is OAuth ?

- OAuth or Open standard for Auhtorization is an open standard for authorization using third party applications.
- **OAuth** is a protocol that allows end users to give access to third party applications to access their resources stored on a server.
- **OAuth** doesn't share password data but instead uses authorization **tokens** to prove an identity between consumers and service providers.
- e.g We can retrieve user account information from Facebook/Google so that we can use it in our application.

Q40. What are advantages OAuth ?

- Giving 3rd party application access to existing resources to avoid duplicating the resources
- Users can use already exusting accounts of Google,Microsoft, Facebook etc. instead of creating new registerations every time
- These trusted websites that authorize users on other applications behalf are called **Identity providers**.
- It is flexible, compatible and designed to work with mobile devices and desktop Applications
- Provides a way to grant limited access in terms of scope and duration

Q41. How to use OAuth ?

The user never need to share his credentials with third party applications.Instead of userid and password the applications use the **access token** to fetch the users data.

Following steps are common no matter which provider we are using.

- Register our application with the provider and **receive a key and a secret**

- Once the user shows his intention to authenticate using the provider our application sends a request to the provider for a **request token**(which is just another set of credentials)
- In the final step our application asks the provider for the **access token**. Once our application receives the **access token** it has access to the users data.

Q42. How to setup Google account using OAuth ?

To use Google account for authentication, we will have to first register our application with Google.

Here are the steps to register your application with Google.

- Once we successfully register our application with Google, we will be given a **Client ID** and **Client Secret**. We need both of these for using Google authentication with our Web API service.
- To register your application go to https://console.developers.google.com

Q43. What is Bearer token in OAuth ?

OAuth protocol supports bearer tokens. Once authorized, using bearer token client can request to access resource

A security token is something that any party in possession of the token (a "bearer") can use to present proof-of-possession .

Protocol defines two types of tokens used in the process

- **Access Token :** These are credentials required to access the protected resources
- **Refresh Token :** Refresh tokens are credentials used to obtain access tokens when it becomes invalid or expires etc.

Q44. What is Access token in OAuth ?

- An **Access Token** is a credential that can be used by an application to **access** an **API**.
- **Access Tokens** can be either an opaque string or a JSON web **token**.
- They inform the **API** that the bearer of the **token** has been authorized to **access** the

  API and perform specific actions specified by the scope that has been granted.

Q45. What are Oauth Grant types ?

Grant is a credential which represents owner's authorization and used by client to access owner's protected resources.

- The **grant_type** URL parameter is required for the /token endpoint, which exchanges a grant for real tokens. So the OAuth2 server knows what you are sending to it. so you must specify it with the value password.
- The **grant_type=password** means that you are sending a username and a password to the **/token endpoint**.

Q46. What are JWT tokens ?

A JSON Web Token (JWT) is a JSON object that is a safe way to represent a set of information between two parties.

The token is composed of :

- a header,
- a payload,
- and a signature.

Simply put, a JWT is just a string with the following format:

header.payload.signature

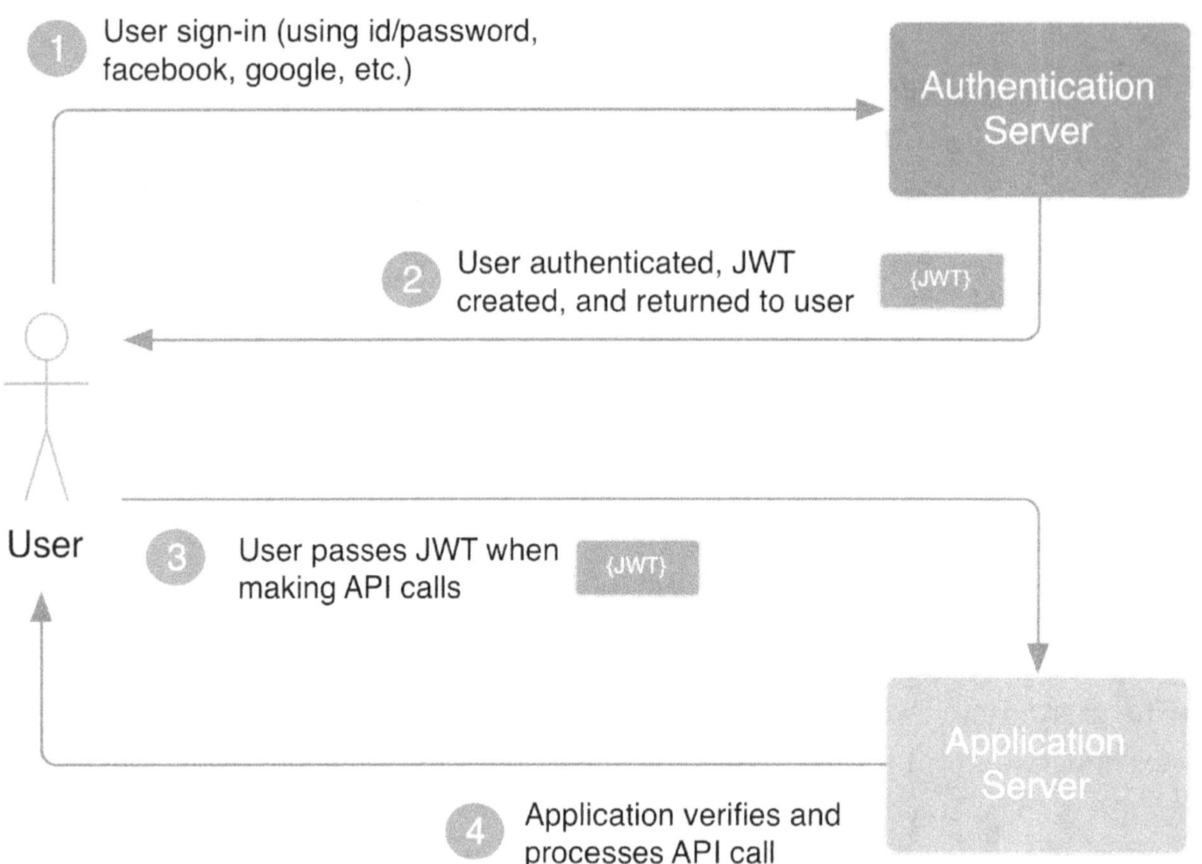

- It relies on signed tokens which are sent by user to server with each request.
- you put all claims in json web structure.
- you sign structure using asymmetric key and encode whole thing in Base64.
- validating signature,issuer and audience

Q47. What is structure of JWT token ?

JWT Structure :

header.payload.signature

Header :-

- alg: Information about type of algorithm which is used like HMAC SHA256 or RSA []
- Typ: type of JWT token e.g. typ:'JWT'

Payload :-

- It contains claims
- claims are user details or additional metadata

:-

- Provide more security

e.g.

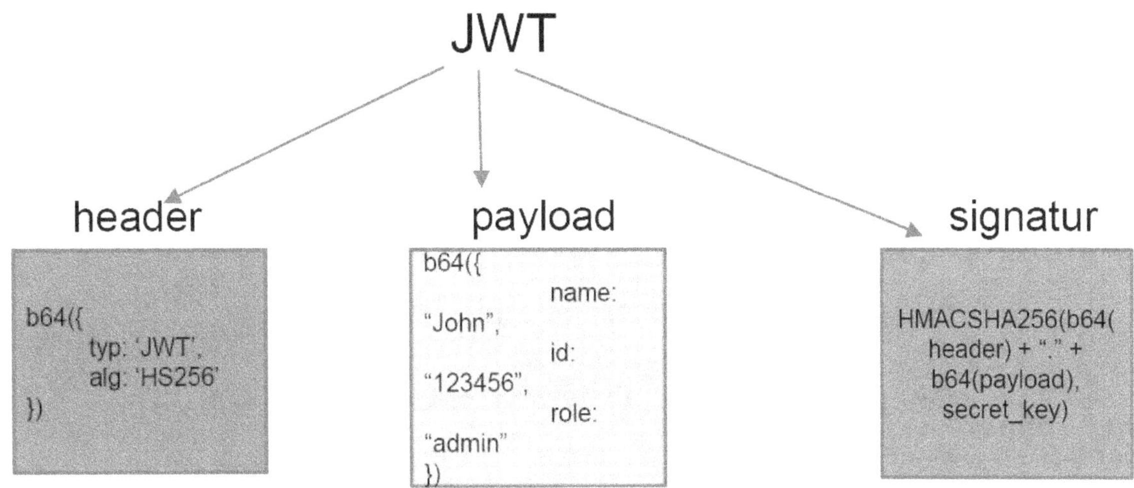

(header.payload.signature)

Q48. What are benefits JWT token ?

- Securely transfer information between any two bodies
- Digitally signed – information is verified and trusted
- Compact – JWT can be send via URL,POST request,HTTP header
- Fast transaction
- Self contained – Contains info about the user
- Avoiding query the database more than once

Q49. What are the steps to create JWT token in Web Api ?

Step1 : Create the HEADER

The header is a JSON object in the following format:

```
{
"typ": "JWT",
 "alg": "HS256"
 }
```

Step 2. Create the PAYLOAD

The payload component of the JWT is the data that's stored inside the JWT

This data is also referred to as the "claims" of the JWT

```
{ "userId": "b08f86af-35da-48f2-8fab-cef3904660bd"}
```

There are several different standard claims for the JWT payload, such as

- "iss" the issuer,
- "sub" the subject, and
- "exp" the expiration time.

Note : Keep in mind that the size of the data will affect the overall size of the JWT

Step 3. Create the SIGNATURE

The signature is computed using the following pseudo code:

```
HMACSHA256 hmac = new HMACSHA256();
string key = Convert.ToBase64String(hmac.Key)
```

Algorithm used : SecurityAlgorithms.HmacSha256Signature

Step 4: Put All Three JWT Components Together

- Now that we have created all three components, we can create the JWT.
- *header.payload.signature* structure of the JWT,
- we simply need to combine the components, with periods (.) separating them.

e.g.

```
// JWT Token
eyJ0eXAiOiJKV1QiLCJhbGciOiJIUzI1NiJ9.eyJ1c2VySWQiOiJiMDhmODZhZi0zNWRhLTQ4Zjl
tOGZhYi1jZWYzOTA0NjYwYmQifQ.-xN_h82PHVTCMA9vdoHrcZxH-x5mb11y1537t3rGzc
M
```

Step 5: Verifying the JWT

- JWT-attached API call to the application, can be validated.

- It matches the JWT signature created by the authentication server.

- If the signatures match, then that means the JWT is valid otherwise invalid.

- So by verifying the JWT, the application adds a layer of trust between itself

  and the user.

Q50. Practical implementation of JWT token in Web Api ?

To use the JWT functionality, you must install a package that offers access to JWT.

System.IdentityModel.Tokens.Jwt package

e.g : [TokenManager.cs - JKT Token Manager class]

```
using Microsoft.IdentityModel.Tokens;

using System;

using System.IdentityModel.Tokens.Jwt;

using System.Security.Claims;

using System.Security.Cryptography;

namespace webApiTokenAuthentication.Models

{

public class TokenManager

{
```

```csharp
public static string Secret = SecretKey();

public static string GenerateToken(string username)

{

byte[] key = Convert.FromBase64String(Secret);

//1. create a SymmetricSecurityKey object by using the HMACSHA256 secret

SymmetricSecurityKey securityKey = new SymmetricSecurityKey(key);

//2.create descriptor object. This represents the main content of the JWT,

//such as the claims, the expiration date and the signing information.

SecurityTokenDescriptor descriptor = new SecurityTokenDescriptor

{

Subject = new ClaimsIdentity(new[] {

new Claim(ClaimTypes.Name, username)}),

Expires = DateTime.UtcNow.AddMinutes(30),

SigningCredentials = new SigningCredentials(securityKey,

SecurityAlgorithms.HmacSha256Signature)

};

//3.Then, the token is created and a string version of it is returned.

JwtSecurityTokenHandler handler = new JwtSecurityTokenHandler();

JwtSecurityToken token = handler.CreateJwtSecurityToken(descriptor);

return handler.WriteToken(token);

}

public static string SecretKey()

{

HMACSHA256 hmac = new HMACSHA256();
```

```
string key = Convert.ToBase64String(hmac.Key);

return key;

}

}

}
```


Filters are used to inject extra logic at the different levels of WebApi Framework request processing. Filters provide a way for cross-cutting concerns (logging, authorization, and caching). Filters can be applied to an action or controller level.

Below are the types of filters in Web API.

Authentication Filter –

An authentication filter helps us to authenticate the user detail. In the authentication filter, we write the logic for checking user authenticity.

Authorization Filter –

Authorization Filters are responsible for checking User Access. They implement the IauthorizationFilter interface in the framework.

Action Filter –

Action filters are used to add extra logic before or after action methods execution. The **OnActionExecuting** and **OnActionExecuted** methods are used to add our logic before and after an action method is executed.

Exception Filter –

An exception filter is executed when a controller method throws any unhandled exception that is not an HttpResponseException exception. The HttpResponseException type is a special case, because it is designed specifically for returning an HTTP response.

Q52. What are ways to handle exception in Web Api ?

We can handle exceptions in following ways :

- Using HttpResponseException
- Using Exception Filters

Using HttpResponseException

This exception class allows us to **return HttpResponseMessage to the client**. It returns HTTP **status code** that is specified in the exception Constructor.

e.g.

```csharp
public string Get(int id)

{

var data = dataList.Where(x => x == id).Count() < 1 ? null : dataList.Where(x => x == id);

if (data == null)

{

var response = new HttpResponseMessage(HttpStatusCode.NotFound)

{

Content = new StringContent($"record not found with key {id}"),

ReasonPhrase = $"[{id} Key Not Found]"

};

throw new HttpResponseException(response);

}

string result = "success";

return result;

}
```

Using Exception Filters

Exception filters can be used to handle unhandled exceptions which are generated in Web API.Note that exception filter does not catch HttpResponseException exception because HttpResponseException is specifically designed to return the HTTP response.
This is an attribute so we can decorate both action method and controller with this. Exception filter is very similar to HandleErrorAttribute in MVC.

- Implement **ExceptionFilterAttribute** in your custom exception class
- Override **OnException**() method

e.g.

public class CustomExceptionFilter : **ExceptionFilterAttribute**

{

public override void **OnException**(HttpActionExecutedContext actionExecutedContext)

{

string exceptionMessage = string.Empty;

if (actionExecutedContext.Exception.InnerException == null)

{

  exceptionMessage = actionExecutedContext.Exception.Message;

}

else

{

  exceptionMessage = actionExecutedContext.Exception.InnerException.Message;

}

//We can log this exception message to the file or database.

```csharp
var response = new HttpResponseMessage(HttpStatusCode.InternalServerError)
{
Content = new StringContent("An unhandled exception was thrown by service."),
ReasonPhrase = "Internal Server Error.Please Contact your Administrator."
};
actionExecutedContext.Response = response;
}
}
//controller class
[CustomExceptionFilter]
[Route("method")]
public string GetMethod()
{
//Todo: task
throw new ArgumentException();
}
```

Q53. What are Authentication Filters in Web Api ?

An authentication filter is a component that authenticates an HTTP request.
Authentication proves the identity of the client.

In Web API, authentication filters implement
the System.Web.Http.Filters.IAuthenticationFilter interface.

The **IAuthenticationFilter** interface has two methods:

- **AuthenticateAsync** authenticates the request by validating credentials in the
  request, if present.

- **ChallengeAsync** adds an authentication challenge to the **HTTP response**, if needed.

e.g.

```csharp
public class CustomAuthentication : Attribute, IAuthenticationFilter

{

public bool AllowMultiple => throw new NotImplementedException();

public async Task AuthenticateAsync(HttpAuthenticationContext context,
CancellationToken cancellationToken)

{

// 1. Look for credentials in the request.

HttpRequestMessage request = context.Request;

AuthenticationHeaderValue authorization = request.Headers.Authorization;

// 2. If there are no credentials, do nothing.

if (authorization == null)

{

return;

}

// 3. If there are credentials but the filter does not recognize the

//   authentication scheme, do nothing.

if (authorization.Scheme != "Basic")

{

return;

}

}

public Task ChallengeAsync(HttpAuthenticationChallengeContext context,
CancellationToken cancellationToken)
```

```
{
//TODO
}
}
```

Q54. What are Authorization Filters in Web Api ?

Authorization determines whether the client can access a particular resource.

- Implement **AuthorizationFilterAttribute** class
- Override **OnAuthorization()** method

e.g.

```csharp
public class AuthorizationHandlerAttribute : AuthorizationFilterAttribute

{

public override void OnAuthorization(HttpActionContext actionContext)

{

string AccessTokenFromRequest = "";

if (actionContext.Request.Headers.Authorization != null)

{

// get the access token

AccessTokenFromRequest =
actionContext.Request.Headers.Authorization.Parameter;

}

string AccessTokenStored = "";

// write some code to get stored access token, probably from database

// then assign the value to a variable for later use

// compare access token
```

```
if (AccessTokenFromRequest != AccessTokenStored)

{

// if the token is not valid then return 401 Http Status

}

}

}
```

Q55. What is CSRF ?

Cross-Site Request Forgery (CSRF) is an attack that forces authenticated users to submit a request to a Web application against which they are currently authenticated.

e.g: An email or link that tricks the victim into sending a forged request to a server. As the unsuspecting user is authenticated by their application at the time of the attack, it's impossible to distinguish a legitimate request from a forged one.

Validation against CSRF :

Add the code to your Views that adds an anti-forgery token to the data that the browser sends back to the server. If you're using HTML Helpers, that code looks like this: **@Html.AntiForgeryToken()**

This method adds the hidden form field and also sets the cookie token.It will add a input field :

```
<input name="__RequestVerificationToken" type="hidden"

value="6fGBtLZmVBZ59oUad1Fr33BuPxANKY9q3Srr5y[...]" />
```

The issue is that, in your HttpPost methods, you need to check that you get that token back. That is easy to do in both ASP.NET MVC and ASP.NET Core: You just add the **ValidateAntiForgeryToken** attribute to your methods.

e.g.

[ValidateAntiForgeryToken]

public void PostData()

{

//todo

}

It would be easier just to add the attribute to your controller class. The problem with that solution is that you'd be incurring the cost of checking for the token with *every* request, not just with the HttpPost methods.

using ASP.NET Core, you can add the AutoAntiForgeryToken to your controller classes, like this:

[AutoAntiForgeryToken]
public class HomeController: Controller

This attribute checks only the dangerous methods (that is, only methods that aren't a GET or one of the other methods you never use: TRACE, OPTIONS and HEAD). You'll get all the protection you need and none that you don't.

Q56. What is XSS ?

Cross-Site Scripting (XSS) is a security vulnerability which enables an attacker to place client side scripts (usually JavaScript) into web pages. When other users load affected pages the attacker's scripts will run, enabling the attacker to steal cookies and session tokens.

By default ASP.NET MVC does not allow a user to submit HTML tags for avoiding Cross-Site Scripting attack to our application.

So to overcome this type of error in MVC applications we have to use "AllowHtml" attribute in our model class.

public class Employee {

[AllowHtml]

public string MessageText { get; set; }

}

The ValidateInput attribute is used to allow sending the HTML content or codes to the server which, by default, is disabled by ASP.NET MVC to avoid XSS (Cross-Site Scripting) attacks. This attribute is used to enable or disable the request validation. By default, request validation is enabled in ASP.NET MVC.

e.g

[HttpPost]

[ValidateInput(false)] // will allow html tags, by default they are not allowed

public string Index(string message) {

return "Your message" + message;

}

Q57. What are threats and how to secure a API ?

Some of the threats and their solutions are : -

Authentication issues

- Threat - Cross- site request forgery [CSRF]
  Cross-Site Request Forgery (CSRF) is an attack where a malicious site sends a request to a vulnerable site where the user is currently logged in
- Solution – [ValidateAntiForgeryToken]

Credentials Mangement

- Threat – Use of hard coded password
- Solution – store passwords out of application code. Best practice to store credentials are in locations such as configuration or properties files

Cross-site scripting (XSS)

- Threat - Xss attacks occur when an attacker uses a web application to send malicious code,generally in the form of a browser side script, to different end user.These attcks succed if application uses untrusted data in the output it generates without validating or encoding it.

- Solution – sanitize all output generated from user-supplied input

Directory traversal

- Threat - External control of file name or path : Allowing user input to control paths in filesystem opearions may enable an attacker to access or modify protected resources
- Solution – validate all user-supplied input to ensure that it confirms to the expected format, using centralized data validation routines. When using black lists, be sure that sanitizing rouitne removes all instances of disallowed characters
- E.g. – cleanse special character in user-supplied filenames.

Insufficient input validation

- Threat - Application receives input from an upstream component that specifies multiple attributes,properties or fields that are to be initialized or updated in an object. By manipulating contents of HTTP request, attacker maybe able to set malicious attributes.
- Solution – Explicitly specify which of the Model's attributes should be accessible using ***Bind attribute*** by setting the Include property to each allowable property and setting the Exclude property to each prohibited property.
- E.g.

```
Public class ModelClass
{
    Public string Name {get;set;}
    Public string LoginType {get;set;}
    Public string Password {get;set;}
}
Public void GetLogin( [Bind(Include = "Name, Password")] ModelClass modelObj )
{
    ......
}
```

Q58. What are HttpHandler and HttpModule in Asp.net ?

Many times we need to inject some kind of logic before the page is requested. Some of the commonly used pre-processing logics are stat counters, URL rewriting, authentication / authorization and many more.

ASP.NET provides two ways of injecting logic in the request pipeline HttpHandlers and HttpModules.

HttpHandler - The Extension Based Preprocessor

- HttpHandler help us to inject pre-processing logic based on the extension of the file name requested.
- So when a page is requested, HttpHandler executes on the base of extension file names and on the base of verbs

HttpModule - The Event Based Preprocessor

- HttpModule is an event based methodology to inject pre-processing logic before any resource is requested.
- When any client sends a request for a resource, the request pipeline emits a lot of events
- Some of the events are : -
- BeginRequest, AuthenticateRequest, AuthorizeRequest, PreRequestHandlerExecute, PostRequestHandlerExecute, EndRequest

Modules are called before and after the handler executes. Modules enable developers to intercept, participate in, or modify each individual request. Handlers are used to process individual endpoint requests. Handlers enable the ASP.NET Framework to process individual HTTP URLs or groups of URL extensions within an application. Unlike modules, only one handler is used to process a request.

HttpHandler	HttpModule
An http handler returns a response to a request that is identified by a file name extension. i.e; .aspx (page handler)	An http module is invoked for all types of requests and responses

It uses IHttpHandler Interface.	It uses IHttpModule Interface.
It is used for rss feeds, image server etc.	it is used for security, logging and custom headers/footers etc.

About the Author

Vishal garg

Vishal Garg is a technical writer with a passion for writing technical books. He has passion for learning new technologies and share the knowledge with everyone. He is well versed in technologies like Azure, Devops, Angular, .Net core, C# etc. He also shares his knowledge with the community through book writings, blog writings , presentations etc.
He has written books on different technologies as well and got a positive reviews on that. He followed a very unique way to cover all major concepts.

With the help of various surveys and real time experience a question bank of a particular topic are compiled and logged in a book.

He is hoping that all readers will be benefited from this book and looking forward to put in more effort to produce quality books in future.

Note : If you like the book, please take some time to put in positive reviews on Amzon website. This feedback will encourage him to produce more quality books in future.

More Books by this Author

- [.Net Core Simplified: Interview QA](#)

- [Angular Simplified: Learning made easy](#)

- [C# Interview Question and Answers: Simplified](#)

- [Azure Devops Interview Questions and Answers](#)

- [Angular 2021: Interview Questions and Answers](#)

- [C# Interview Questions and Answers : Edition:2021](#)

www.ingramcontent.com/pod-product-compliance
Lightning Source LLC
Chambersburg PA
CBHW080852160726
47999CB00009B/3095